DATA
della misu

Meat Salt Time
Salumi Master Cristiano Creminelli

Creative Director: Gemma Gatti
Author: Tony Seichrist
Editor: Tania Rochelle
Photographer: Artem Nazarov
Designer: Annabel Mangold
Mech Artist: Christine Sutton
Illustration: Clay Pullen

PC Press

Published by PC Press
Atlanta, Georgia

First Edition
ISBN: 978-0-9846089-0-4

MEAT
SALT
TIME

SALUMI MASTER
CRISTIANO CREMINELLI

Tony Seichrist

Acknowledgments:

I would like to thank Christine, Jerry, Dong Soo, Melissa, and Gemma
for helping make PC Press a reality. I would also like to thank Tania
Rochelle; your commitment to this book was truly amazing. Thank you.

Special thanks to Peter Bowerman; your insights provided us with the
tools and the confidence to move forward.

Thanks to Clay Pullen for coming through in a pinch.

Much gratitude to Linton Hopkins of restaurant eugene and Tommy
Searcy of Gum Creek Farms for allowing me to pick your giant brains.

To Cristiano's brother Andrea and his fiance Angela; to Cristiano's
mother and father, Rosarita and Umberto; to Enrico Porrino, and to all
the Creminelli family and those at Salumificio, your kindness while
hosting us was unequaled. I hope to soon repay the hospitality you
showed us in Biella.

To Nico, Valentina, and Francesca of Il Talucco, thank you for sharing
your wonderful home and fantastic food and wine with us. We cannot
wait to return.

To Chris Bowler, Jared Lynch, Don Allphin Jr., and the staff of
Creminelli Fine Meats, thanks for your patience and wisdom, and for
putting up with our being underfoot. Without you, none of this would
have been possible.

To the Caputos, our greatest appreciation for helping Creminelli Fine
Meats come to be. You championed a truly great cause.

And finally, to my own family, the Gattis and the Verrillos: I am so
fortunate to have been raised among those who made good food a
ceaseless adventure. Thank you.

Biella, Italy — where it all began

In the past twenty-five years the United States has borne a slow, quiet revolution in food making. Artisan has become the buzzword, and I've thought long and hard about what this means for the food we sell at Murray's. It's a complicated conversation, and for us it's become an amalgam of several facets: first and foremost, it's about taste. The best food, it seems, is the most direct. The best ingredients – a short list – guided by an adherence to, and an embracing of, traditional technique. Real food requires serious craftsmanship. There's nothing to hide behind. There aren't additives or fancy "modern" stabilizers and fillers. I shy away from government-mandated criteria like "organic" and "all-natural." When I first tasted the cured salami Cristiano Creminelli makes, it was a wondrous discovery.

Liz Thorpe — Vice President, Murray's Cheese, NY, NY, author of The Cheese Chronicles

What I learned from Cristiano is that salami, like all food, is a distinctly regional craft. Most Americans know the style of Genoa, and the southern Italian interpretations brought by immigrants from Calabria and Sicily. Those intensely hot regions produced a quickly acidified meat. Namely, it has bite. Tangy, twangy, mouth-watering bite in a dense, tough, mouthful. A man's salami, as I fondly regard it. But here was something new. A velvety texture meant, I thought, a problem. In fact it is the distinct signature of northern Piemonte where Cristiano studied with his father and grandfather; there, a pillowy texture was the aplomb of perfection.

Over the past two years we have been fortunate enough to share with our patrons the wondrous results of Cristiano's experiments. There was the first white truffle salami, with creeping, tentative notes of that rare, seasonal fungus. A Barolo interpretation didn't just incorporate wine, but insisted on the most precious Nebbiolo-based red of Creminelli's home turf, and with it delivered a musky, luscious flavor that managed to capture and elevate the already supreme pork.

In these days of food TV and bloggers, restaurant charcuterie boards, and home curers, I hear a lot about artisan food. What is rare is to find someone with one foot firmly planted in a deep and personal tradition, and the other foot stretching far forward to create a new and singular practice. I've been told that Cristiano will sleep in his cure rooms, waking every few hours to gently prod and turn his evolving creations. I imagine a kind of ancient, molecular exchange in those damp, quiet hours. There is a bridge between three generations of knowledge and instinct, and a small, perfect food that some person, somewhere, will be privileged enough to taste. In his backward looking motions, Cristiano Creminelli is changing the food Americans can experience.

Without honesty in food,
there are only gimmicks,
tricks played on the
consumer. It is up to chefs
and artisans to pursue
quality that surpasses their
own standards, not just those
of their customers.

Tony Seichrist — Atlanta, Georgia

I began my cooking career at Five and Ten, a popular little restaurant in Athens, Georgia. After two-and-a-half intense and somewhat blurry years working my way around that kitchen, I applied for a chef position, opening a small farm-fed restaurant in the community of Serenbe, in an old inn on 1,000 acres on the outskirts of Atlanta.

The small scale and relaxed pace of Serenbe allowed me the freedom to use an extremely high percentage of local ingredients. My focus as a chef changed; I began to look for the best, freshest product I could find, and I would do as little to it as possible. I'd gut fresh trout right before tossing it, still thrashing, into the frying pan. I also played with various bacon recipes and smoking methods, but it wasn't until I moved to Italy to study cooking that I truly began to understand the difference between an artisan and the rest of us.

In my classes in Italy, we tasted vast amounts of local fare. We'd have oil tastings, salami tastings, and wine tastings, all before lunch. I learned a lot in the classroom, but my real education happened when we visited a surprising little salumi shop buried in the remote hills of Le Marche. When we arrived, loopy from the bus ride, we stepped out to find a small, two-pump gas station and convenience store. We were tired from the trip and less than impressed with the store's shabby exterior. As we entered the small wooden door we were greeted cordially by an ancient Italian couple who processed the local hogs and made salumi to sell in this small, odd place. *We had stepped back in time.*

He then produced a young salami, which he peeled, sliced and smeared on the hot bread.

This was when I first realized how practical and essential to life salami had been in the recent past, when each family raised a few pigs and turned them into cured whole muscle cuts and salami to preserve for the year to come. Fresh pork was hardly ever eaten and was usually reserved for the wealthy. The seeds of my love affair with salumi were planted that day. It would blossom during a spur-of-the-moment excursion to Florence with a fellow classmate.

We loaded our packs into my crappy rent-a-car and, after a bit of discussion regarding how long it had been since he'd sat behind the wheel and how nostalgic he was for that feeling of power on the open road, he persuaded me to let him drive. We started for Florence and managed to make the rainy highway, which seemed to be quite an accomplishment for him. Everything was fine, if a little shaky, until the tunnel. At the entrance, the car nicked an exceptionally high curb and blew a tire.

After plunking along to the other end, we managed to pull off onto the soggy grass shoulder to inspect the damage. It was significant, involving not just the tire but the wheel as well. My companion — a former Israeli soldier — informed me that he'd never changed a tire, so I took the lead. After I'd raised the car up about three inches, the soft soil began shifting the base and bending the jack. It took two cold, wet hours of rigging limbs and roadside debris to dig and wedge our way out, but we managed to free ourselves. Filthy and grumpy, we continued down the road to the next exit.

As it happened, the next exit was for the Frasassi Caves, an enormous cave system discovered in the 1970s. We pulled into the parking lot and walked around the small booths and shops. We came across an old man selling salami, sweets, and coffee. We chatted for a few minutes, and he insisted on making us something special, since we were wet and covered in mud and apparently looked pitiful. He began by toasting a few thick crostini and rubbing them with fresh garlic. He then produced a young salami, which he peeled, sliced, and smeared on the hot bread. I'm not sure if it was because I was drenched and muddy, or because I'd purchased the rental insurance, or, more likely, because of the incomparable flavor, but this was one of the top ten best things I have ever eaten.

We continued stuffing our crumb-covered mouths as he explained that this was wild boar salami with black truffles found in the hills around the caves. He had collected the truffles and shot the boar himself. It was then that I got it. I finally understood what all the fuss was about.

I finished school, packed up my tattered borrowed car, and started driving towards Puglia. I ate my way down southern Italy and back up again before I returned home. Back in the States, I was offered a job at Holeman and Finch in Atlanta. The majority of my time there went into producing whole hog charcuterie, which I tried to learn on the fly.

I read every book and experimented with every possible variable. However, I was keenly aware of the fact that I had failed to master the art at all. I'd merely produced an edible product that was tasty enough for a provincial clientele. I had good recipes, but I wasn't in total control of my process or my curing cell environment. This failure stuck in my mind and, like a stubborn itch, refused to go away.

I searched for artisans, tasted products, and wrote countless emails, but I was continually disappointed. I could not recreate the salami experience I'd had in Italy — until we discovered Creminelli Fine Meats. It was like finding your wallet long after giving up on ever finding it. When the package I'd ordered from Salt Lake City arrived, I hoped to find evidence of a true salami artisan in the USA. I found a master instead.

The first time I met Cristiano in person, it was early fall, and I had flown out to Utah to visit. I began by interviewing his partners, Jared and Chris. Jared handles the business operations, while Chris manages the sales and marketing. I started asking them questions about Cristiano and how he worked.

They both emphatically impressed upon me his ability to predict the data that their testing machines would later report. The FDA requires the salami be tested by machines that record such things as the pH and water levels. Although he adheres strictly to all the rules, Cristiano really needs no machines. "He knows what the test says before the test does," Chris told me, just by touching, smelling, and looking at his salamis and their environment. Cristiano has learned to observe certain sense-oriented cues and what they mean for the salami aging process. This incredible knowledge and familiarity with the salami making process makes Cristiano Creminelli the premier salami maker in the US.

Creminelli Fine Meats is a relatively young company, but it embodies the quality, standards, and rich culinary heritage borne of the 400- year-old Creminelli tradition. Cristiano is working within the strict US industry regulations and creating an artisinal product that far exceeds the typical niche market distributions.

1

THE ZAMPONE

Americans were hungry
for real salami.

THE ZAMPONE

The first inkling Cristiano ever had about starting a salami factory in America came to him during a visit to New York. He and his brother Andrea were walking down Madison Avenue and happened to pass a high-end Italian specialty shop. In the window there was a stuffed pig's foot on display, with a price tag of $58 per pound.

They were struck by the cost of this item, called Zampone. In Italy, it is an inexpensive peasant dish that is boiled and stuffed with the same scrap-rich mixture as Cotechino. Imagine peddling ham hocks as a delicacy. This was the moment he realized the potential of his trade in America.

In Italy, the market for his salami is limited. Every town has a salumi maker who has a loyal following and adheres to local regional traditions. The importation laws of the US make it impossible to ship dry-cured fermented salami directly. Hence, the only logical way to expand would be to open a shop in the United States. The US was like the Promised Land, a massive untapped market with no regional boundaries and a population looking—and willing to pay—for something better.

Later, when he met Chris Bowler, the inkling turned into an ambition. During the initial startup, Tony Caputo's Market and Deli, a specialty shop in Salt Lake City, allowed Cristiano to put several curing cells in their basement and named him their official in-house salami maker.

He started by making small batches by himself, butchering, grinding, stuffing, and tying everything, then hanging it at Caputo's. This allowed Cristiano to begin building his name and reputation locally, even before he moved into his own factory. "Without Caputo's, there would be no Creminelli Fine Meats," Cristiano professes.

CREMINELLI

*I was practically born
in a salumificio.*

Marzo 1906

Old Salumificio opens.

28 Agosto 1939

My father Umberto Creminelli is born in Biella, Italy.

1 Luglio 1942

My grandfather Ugo Landinelli is nominee chef for General Badoglio.

2 Novembre 1968

A big flood happens in Biella province and we stop production for six days. Twelve people die in our town.

24 Novembre 1968

My father marries my mother Rosarita Landinelli on this day.

9 Novembre 1969

I am born the same day as my grandfather, Giacomo Creminelli.

Settembre 1975

We start to use pork meat from the special pig "suino pesante piemontese."

15 Giugno 1984

New Salumificio opens.

17 Agosto 1978

My brother Andrea is born.

1 Luglio 1995

My wedding day. Silvia and I chose that day because one night I had a dream of my grandma, who had already passed, and she told me the date of my marriage. Our daughter Camilla was born in 2000.

THE FAMILY

We had the pleasure of traveling to Biella to watch the centuries-old tradition firsthand at the Creminelli family's Salumificio diVigliano. Upon arrival, we were introduced to our host, translator, and tour guide, Enrico Porrino. Enrico is an exceptionally warm and kind lifelong friend of the Creminelli's.

During our tour of Salumificio, the salumi makers continued diligently at their tasks, stopping only to allow us to take photos or get a better view. The smell of the air was almost identical to the factory in Salt Lake City; its combination of mold, meat, and spices flooded me with deja vu. Enrico introduced me to a veteran member of the crew, who quickly told me in Italian that he was the one who "taught Cristiano everything he knows." Watching the speed and skill with which the elderly man worked, I could believe his claim.

As for the family itself, each member has an area of expertise that seems to stem from his personality. Cristiano's brother, Andrea, an overt people person, is the business representative and deals directly with the whole-sale customers. Andrea and Cristiano look alike and share their father's quick wit, but Andrea is rowdy and expansive, while Cristiano, the salumi master, is more focused and scientific. Their father, Umberto, is the source of each son's distinct qualities, a wise and experienced balance of the two; he crunches numbers and oversees all aspects of Salumificio, his small, thin cigarette glowing between his fingers.

In Italy, I was able to get a better sense of the customs and knowledge that had been painstakingly accumulated by generations and proven by years of trial and error. Salumificio diVigliano is the definition of a family business, and the heirloom methods and recipes required to master the art are guarded like a priceless treasure. This was where Cristiano grew up, the environment that molded and shaped one of the finest artisans in the world.

Salt Lake City

When I first asked Cristiano why he chose to open his shop in Utah, he blew out a long breath and said, "Wow, that is a long story." Nothing is ever simple — and certainly not starting a new company in a foreign country. The short answer to the question is relationships. Creminelli Fine Meats is so much more than just a curing facility, and it has taken many amazing people to make it everything it is today.

During the Olympics in Torino, Cristiano met Chris Bowler, now the president of Creminelli Fine Meats. Chris was working in Italy as Regional Director of the Utah International Business Development Office and Official Liaison for the US Olympic Committee. While looking for vendors to help supply the Committee, Chris came across Salumificio diVigliano. Chris and Cristiano struck up a friendship and, eventually, together hatched a plan to bring exceptional quality, and traditionally accurate, salami to America.

After a period of researching possible locations, they whittled down their list to a few places in the Pacific Northwest and Rocky Mountain areas. Chris's connections in Utah put Salt Lake City at the top of the list right away, but it was the strange similarity in climate to Biella that made it stand out.

Climate-wise, Salt Lake City is the American version of Biella. Like Biella, Salt Lake is balanced and consistent. The cool, dry air coming through the mountains is much like the Alpine winds that blow into northern Italy. It is the climate Cristiano has worked in all his life, the one wherein he learned to fully express his mastery of salami. Utah's predictable climate plays to Cristiano's strengths, and, with a craft that relies on using climate to control microbial life, nothing could be more important. It was a bonus that Salt Lake and Biella shared other vital characteristics. Biella is nestled at the base of an ancient mountain, with a gin-clear river that runs through the middle of town. In Utah, Creminelli Fine Meats sits directly at the foot of a younger mountain chain, which is sliced by blue, snow-fed rivers and streams. Cristiano could feel at home there.

Climate-wise, Salt Lake City is the American version of Biella.

3

THE ABBATOIR &
THE SALUMI HOG

I have my father's job.

In Italy, everyone does.

THE ABBATOIR &
THE SALUMI HOG

The last time I visited Cristiano, I had the opportunity to accompany him to a nearby slaughterhouse, where a local farmer allowed Cristiano to get a very close look at his Black Berkshire hogs before and after slaughter.

It was a thrill to witness Cristiano in this environment, outside the stark whiteness and steel of the factory. I've never seen anyone so excited about pigs. Dressed in a hoodie and his bright red and green Adidas, he truly looked like a kid in a candy store. In this particular case, he was doing some product research for a limited seasonal batch of salami.

"We will be using the whole animal, so it needs to be just right."

He was searching for a heritage breeder close by to supply him with a different type of hog that was completely local. Cristiano uses close to 7,000 pounds of pork weekly, so for his standard salami and sausage lines, he uses a larger supplier that raises Duroc hogs. The tremendous range found in domestic and semi domestic swine is clearly evident in meat quality and carcass structure and is an important variable in salumi making. Certain breeds have qualities suited to whole hog salumi production, where all parts of the hog can be utilized in preservation. This is where the different characteristics of the Old World style and the New World style animals become important.

As we entered through the double doors on to the main floor of the slaughterhouse, the gleaming combination of machinery, blood, and steam was overpowering. There was a respectful clinical efficiency to the men carrying out the task at hand; the speed and precision with which they performed seemed to benefit the animal as well as prevent waste and contamination.

Cristiano began inspecting the freshly hung carcasses, and I followed behind him, taking notes and watching him judge specific attributes. He explained that fat color and quality play a huge role in how a whole carcass can be utilized for salami making. Creminelli Fine Meats does not currently carry whole muscle cuts, so good utilization of the entire hog

It's just a way of life.

The first time he understood the reality of his family's profession, Cristiano was still a young boy.

He remembers the day was so foggy, *you needed a knife.*

He recalls the smell: pig, blood, meat. *Pungente.*

for salami is important. He checked the whiteness and thickness of the belly and back fat, as well as the fat development in the hams. He commented on the rich red color the Berkshire is known for. "This color meat makes beautiful salami," he said, admiring the split carcasses. We watched as the crew continued to do their work, calmly utilizing practiced techniques and powerful hoists to handle the extremely heavy whole animals.

I followed as Cristiano made his way into the cold cutting room, smiling and greeting the guys working the blades. They were all too happy to pose for a photo with their tools before resuming their work, not missing a step. They quickly and cleanly reduced the halved carcasses into primals, then into sub primals, and sorted them accordingly.

Cristiano talked more about pigs all over the world and the types that he used in Biella. "You know, I like the pork in the US better. It is possible to find great pigs in Italy, but maybe not enough for Salumificio." He feels very lucky to be able to buy only Duroc sirloin for his salami, because in Italy it is not possible to buy the same quantity of that particular cut. The evolution of the pork industry has thrown a curve ball to the salumi makers of the world. The long-term selective breeding towards a leaner animal has resulted in animals that don't necessarily do well in salumi production.

The movement from a larding animal to a lean bacon style animal has reduced the marbling and the fat cap capacity of hogs, drying and lightening the meat. Not all varieties have been bred entirely lean, but almost all have been changed by this trend. Breeds like the old line Duroc, Ossabaw, Mangalitsa, and the Pata Negra are examples of older breeds that have seen less of an impact on their genetic makeup; however, the scarcity of some of these lines makes their futures uncertain.

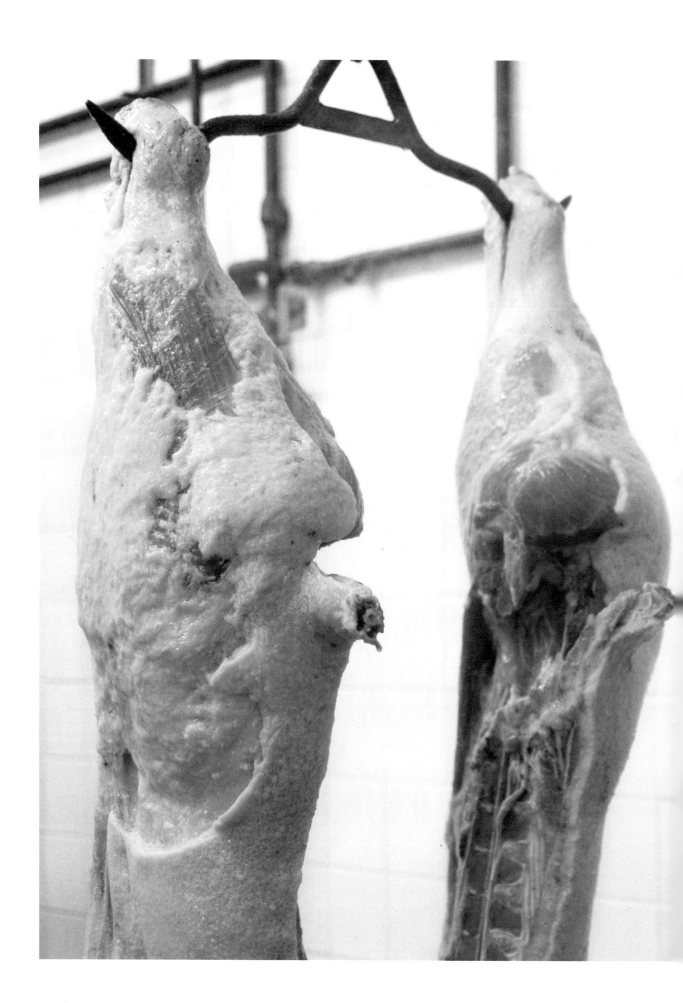

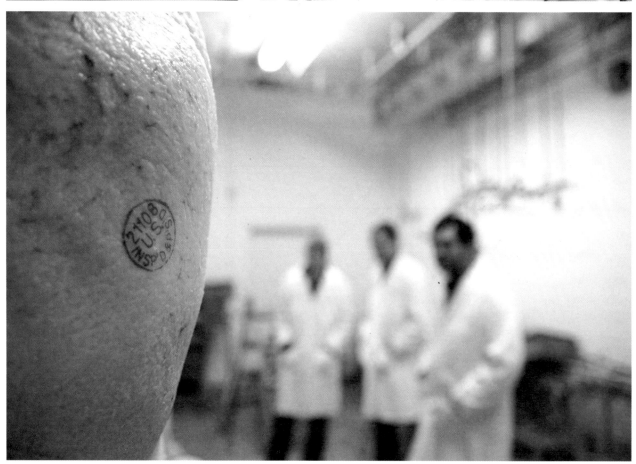

PIG PARTS

Neck
This meat is exclusively reserved for the grinder.

Shoulder
The entire shoulder is perfect sausage cut for small batches. However, it is usually broken down into its two more common forms, the picnic shoulder and the Boston butt, and used for roasts. One shoulder has roughly 80 percent lean and 20 percent fat.

This ratio is perfect for most sausage and salami making. The shoulder may also contain a portion or all of the "coppa," depending on your butcher. The coppa is a roughly shaped cylinder of deeply marbled muscle, with the perfect natural balance of fat and lean.

Belly

Pork belly makes up the fatty portion of the animal and is well known from common applications such as bacon or pancetta, an herbaceous Italian cured and rolled belly. The high quality of belly fat makes it highly desired in salami making. It is also fast becoming a favorite cult ingredient among chefs who use various slow cooking techniques to highlight the tremendous range of flavor and texture that the belly has to offer.

Loin

The general loin portion of the pig covers the back of the animal, from behind the shoulder to the ham. This area can be broken down into several cuts, including sirloin, pork chops, baby back ribs, center loin, blade end, rib end, and tenderloin. The majority of the loin is primarily used for fresh chops, but the sirloin at the end of the loin is versatile and can be eaten fresh or ground and used as the lean portion in salami.

The flavor comes from both the diet of the animal and the climate in which it is cured.

Ham

Everybody knows what the ham is! However, most Americans are familiar with the sweet, crunchy, glazed hams or the standard cooked deli hams but not the hams that live in the dreams of true ham aficionados. Hams are the Pinot Noir of meat, in that they tend to represent the best and the worst of how they were preserved. They take on certain characteristics based on how they were aged, and this is manifested in the quality of the final product.

Hams usually undergo some open-air exposure time in the warmer months, so fresh air and microorganisms gently craft subtle undertones of flavor. The Italian varieties of prosciutto are clear examples of how regions produce unique products that cannot be duplicated outside of their home. The Spanish Bellota hams are made from semi-wild pigs that graze the "Dehesa," a mixed terrain of pastures and five species of oaks that drop their acorns consecutively, ensuring an extremely long-lasting food source for the pigs. These hams are considered to be of the highest quality in the world and have a signature nuttiness all their own. The flavor comes from both the diet of the animal and the climate in which it is cured and aged.

Jowl

The jowl is a fantastically and uniquely marbled area primarily used in making guanciale. Because a pig chews almost constantly, the jowl develops special character and marbling patterns not seen in any other part of the pig.

Shanks

The shanks of a hog extend from above the hock to below the shoulder or ham cut. Shanks receive large amounts of work, ensuring extremely flavorful meat. However, shanks require slow, extended cooking, allowing ample time for softening.

Hocks

The hocks are found from the wrist to the hoof and are most often salted and smoked and used as a flavoring component. In Italy, they treat the pig foot rather differently, hollowing out the hock free of bones and stuffing it before boiling.

BOSTON
BUTT

NECK

JOWL

SHOULDE

PICNIC
SHOULDER

SHAN

HOC

Duroc Pig

LARDO

SIRLOIN

BLADE END

RIB END

CENTER LOIN

TENDERLOIN

RIBS

HAM

BELLY

SHANK

How to break down a hog

Most hogs coming from the processor will usually be split in two. However, in some cases, the pigs will be whole. There are many different ways of breaking down a whole pig. The simple approach is to use a saw and break the animal down into more manageable primals. Generally, the pig is split down the backbone at least to the head. Begin sawing just in front of the ham and hip, taking care to cut straight. You will be sawing through the backbone just north of the hip and the end of the tenderloin.

The rules don't change, just the meat.

Continue to cut behind the front shoulder with the saw, and separate the middle. The middle can be disassembled into the loin, tenderloin, belly, and ribs with just two more saw cuts and a little knife work. Saw the shoulder clean of the head and jowls. That will leave you with two hams with socket and hoof, two bellies, two loin racks, two small rib ends, two tenderloins, two shoulders on the hoof, and one head with jowls. These are the most basic parts of whole hog breakdown. From here it is possible to carve out just about anything.

The salumi maker is in the position to break down the animal as it will best benefit his shop, and how he does it will depend on whether he needs fresh cuts, sausage, terrines, aged hams, guanciale, or pancetta. He is able to plan ahead and modify his cutting technique to best suit his purpose. I will not go into details about this here, but I do want to stress that there is no one perfect approach. Flexibility and a practical understanding of basic swine anatomy are far more important.

A grill cook once told me, "Butchery is just separating meat and connective tissue. If you can break down one animal, you can break down another." Whatever the animal, it will follow a symmetrically and biologically reminiscent form. The rules don't change, just the meat. The first few times you work with a whole animal carcass, take a moment to study it and notice how it changes with movement. By really understanding how the animal "works," you can work more intuitively with your knife.

GRINDING

Meat is everything. Food of my engine,
my energy, my life.

GRINDING

Grinding in the Creminelli production facility is a surprisingly simple procedure. Their process begins with the correct selection of pork cuts that adequately fill their lean and fat requirements. Cristiano's grinding is a three-step process executed in a cold room.

The first step is cutting the fat, or the belly, he uses as the fatty portion of the salami recipe. He cuts the belly into approximately four-inch squares to even the size and ready it for the buffalo chopper. Cristiano usually chooses sirloin for the lean portion of his recipes. However, when using specialty hogs, procured whole, he also uses the hams, shoulders, and necks.

Once all the meat is in relatively large cubes, the lean meat and fat go into the buffalo chopper briefly to reduce the cubes to about one fourth the original size. The speed in which this is done is absolutely crucial to the integrity of the fat and, to a lesser extent, the lean as well. If done quickly, the meat and fat encounter less friction and heat while being reduced. If you have ever tried to dice bacon that wasn't really cold, you know the fundamental problem I am speaking of. The fat melts and becomes elastic and impossible to cut evenly.

Keeping the meat cold is the first priority, but don't forget to use enough tool to do the job quickly. Cristiano excels in this area; he and his team are able to calmly and smoothly execute a precarious task with a combination of the right equipment and well-practiced hands. After the meat and fat are buffalo chopped together, the mixture goes through a coarse grind plate one time. At this point,the meat is ready for seasoning and salt.

Meat Grinder Parts

1. Crank wheel: provides the necessary leverage to grind meat by hand.

2. Housing & Piston: the piston must be cleaned thoroughly to prevent malfunction. This vital piece of machinery allows for air to be removed from the meat mix prior to stuffing.

3. Meat Canister: batch size will primarily dictate the size canister you will need for the job.

4. Stuffer Tip: dictates the size of the tube you will choose. Keep the end wet prior to loading the casings to properly lubricate.

5. Grind Plate: dictates the consistency of the grind: the larger the holes, the chunkier the mix. Experimenting with grind plate sizes is an easy way to vary the bite and texture of your meat.

6. Blade: proper blade maintenance ensures even cuts. Keeping the blade very cold and sharp before use helps reduce heat buildup and prevents smearing.

7. Auger: this is the implement that grabs the meat and forces it forward through the grind plate. This process creates a lot of friction, so chilling the auger is very important.

8. Meat Grinder

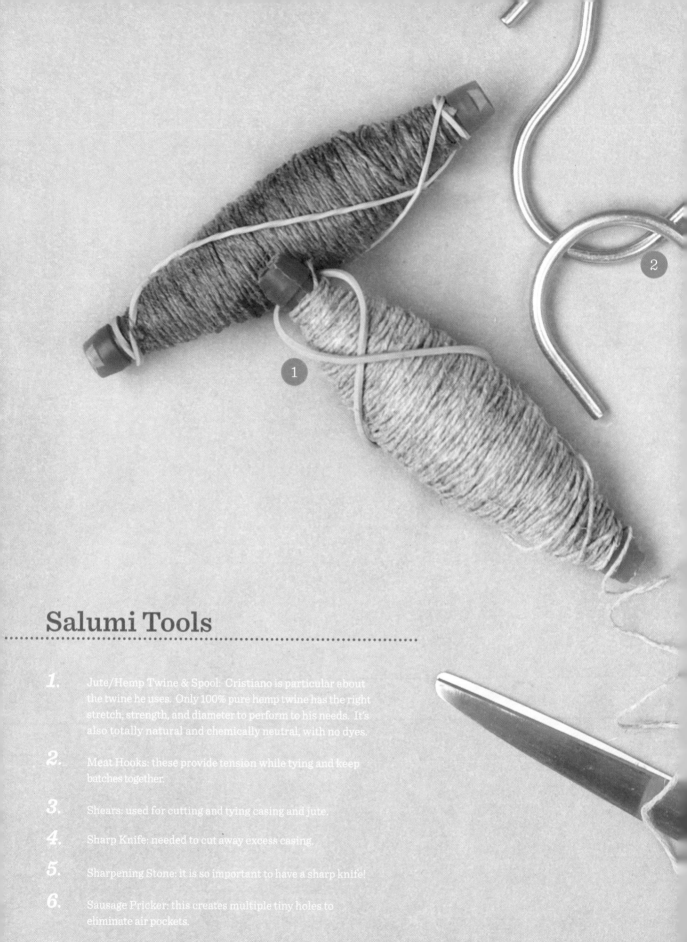

Salumi Tools

....

1.   Jute/Hemp Twine & Spool: Cristiano is particular about the twine he uses. Only 100% pure hemp twine has the right stretch, strength, and diameter to perform to his needs. It's also totally natural and chemically neutral, with no dyes.

2.   Meat Hooks: these provide tension while tying and keep batches together.

3.   Shears: used for cutting and tying casing and jute.

4.   Sharp Knife: needed to cut away excess casing.

5.   Sharpening Stone: it is so important to have a sharp knife!

6.   Sausage Pricker: this creates multiple tiny holes to eliminate air pockets.

7.   White Vinegar: Soak your jute in water and vinegar to soften fibers.

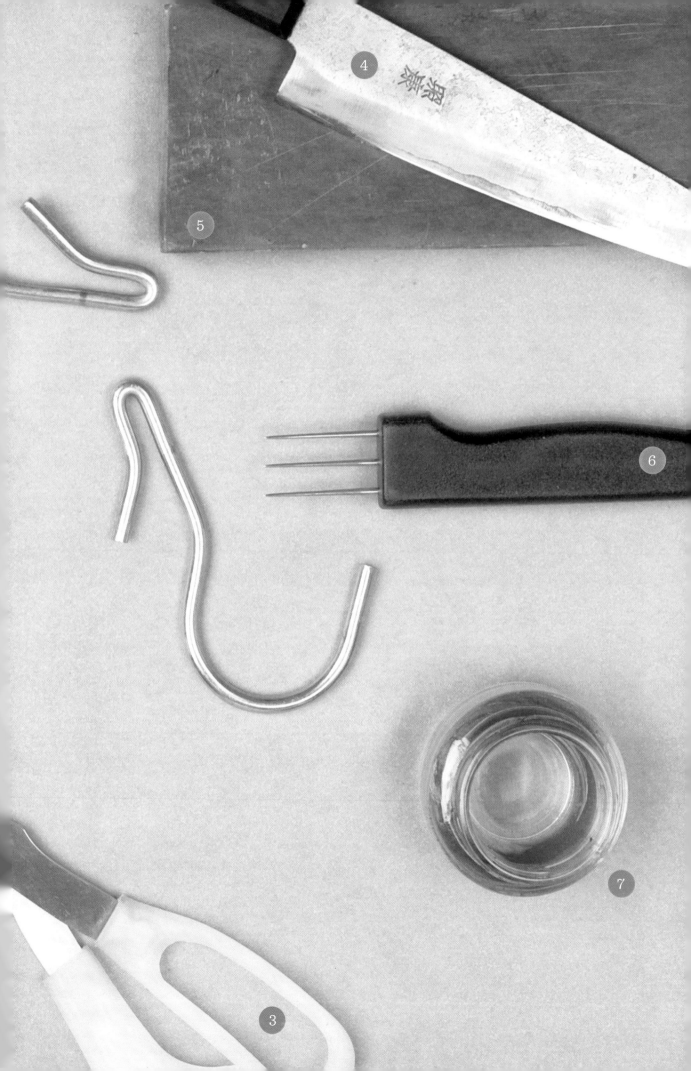

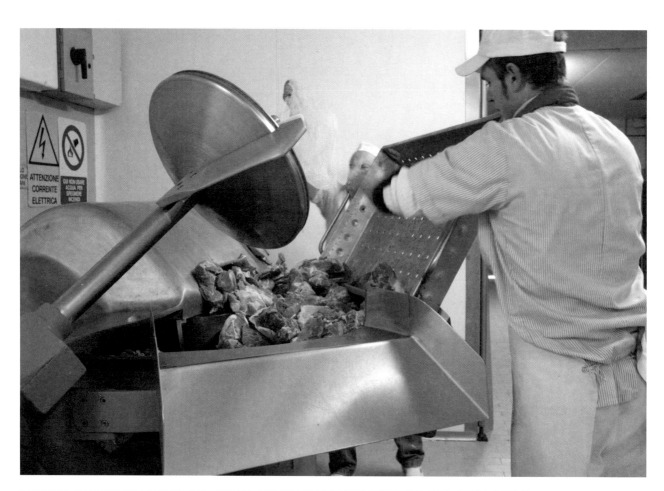

5

SALT, SUGAR & SPICE

Salt is like currency.

SALT

Salt is a cornerstone ingredient in salami and serves several functions. Because it's so important, Cristiano is emphatic about his salt choice: "Salt is an underestimated ingredient. You can't use just any salt. You have to know what's in it." Cristiano uses sea salt and only sea salt.

You can't use just any salt.

He knows that what is inside of the sea salt is stable and pure. He can predict how it will perform in all of his batches.

One day, while sitting in his office after eight hours of stuffing and tying 5,000 pounds of salami, Cristiano gave me a lesson: He began by pulling out a giant chunk of mined Utah salt. I was blown away by the particular slab; it had multi-colored marbled shelves, which he informed me were all different mineral deposits. He pointed to a green layer, saying, "Here is copper." He continued to point out different layers with "silver, iron, and magnesium…" I learned that all these elements can influence the life inside and outside the salami. The natural properties of silver make it an effective antibacterial surface, so when it is infused with salt, the salt carries the elemental signature throughout the salami. At this point the element usually disturbs the culture enough to severely change the salami. Any variable added in this process can inadvertently flaw the salami, and since salt is such a fantastic carrier, it is imperative to control those variables. As far as the quantity of salt, Cristiano says that it can vary slightly based on the other ingredients, but it never exceeds three percent.

Salt

1. Il Sale dei Papa
2. Noto Suzu Shio
3. Bolivian Rose
4. Peruvian Pink
5. Mined Utah Shards
6. Black Cyprus
7. Kala Namak

Salt Colors/ Minerals

Magnesium
Grey

Copper
Green

Cobalt
Blue

Sulphur
Yellow or Black

Calcium
Pink

Iron
Orange

Sugar & Spice

Cristiano is an artist of nuance. He gently coaxes subtle hints of flavors that elegantly pair with the taste of the aging process and don't cover it up. Less experienced salami makers use more intense spices to cover mistakes made in their own products' curing phases. Cristiano has nothing to hide. He starts with his base recipes, the Felino, the Sopressata/Cacciatore, and the Casalingo. Into these three mother recipes he incorporates new flavor profiles. He uses whole organic spices that he grinds himself, as needed, to maximize flavor and freshness.

Nutmeg is Cristiano's single most important spice, a legacy of the trade traditions between Liguria and Piemonte.

Black Pepper is used whole primarily as eye candy, but it also provides intense flashes of heat. White Pepper is the work-horse that provides the bulk of the pepper profile. Dextrose is a simple sugar and the primary food source for the culture. It is consumed very quickly and is easily digested, so remember this if trying to manipulate the length of the life of the culture.

Nutmeg is Cristiano's single most important spice, a legacy of the trade traditions between Liguria and Piemonte. Calabrese Chiles are added to create the Piccante. Cinnamon is sometimes used in salami, but it is used more often in whole muscle cuts. Juniper is ground in-house and is used to give a subtle, earthen, woodsy flavor.

1

2

3

4

Spices

6

STUFFING & TYING

Artisans create with their hands,
not for fortune, but for love.

STUFFING & TYING

One of the highlights of my research for this book was seeing the skill and precision at work in the stuffing and tying process. All the team had assembled in the morning to stuff and tie almost 6,000 pounds of salami and were stationed at white work surfaces with their tool kits.

Cristiano began operating the industrial vacuum stuffer to fill the Felino mix into the beef middle casings. The Felino is almost twice as long as the other varieties and requires a practiced hand to stuff.

After watching Cristiano operate the machine so effortlessly, I was confident that I could handle it with no problem. I had stuffed hundreds and hundreds of salamis, and I figured the super-sized stuffer would only make it easier. So when Cristiano offered me a chance to try it, I eagerly accepted. The shock I felt when I first used this powerful machine was similar to what I felt the first time I fired a rifle. Nothing prepared me for the speed and force.

Stuffing all those salamis felt like firing a BB gun compared to pulling the trigger on this shotgun. I must have wasted a case's worth of salami.

I quickly relinquished the machine and picked up my video camera instead. I proceeded to record the events. An unruffled Cristiano filled each casing with the maximum amount of tension short of rupture, while constantly moistening the extruder tip to prevent breakage. The stuffed casings were grabbed by the waiting staff and were taken back to their work surfaces. Each station included a bucket full of jute-wrapped spools soaking in water with a few tablespoons of white vinegar, a hook, and a metal peg made into the board.

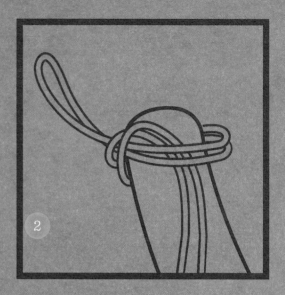

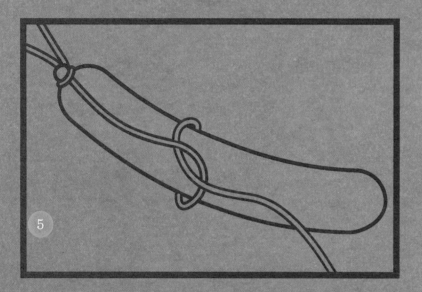

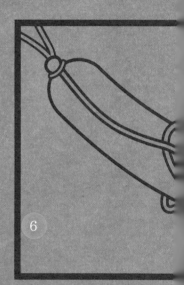

Prep the tying station by soaking the hemp twine spool in hot water. This gives the twine the correct stretching and knotting properties. **1.** Begin by making a six-inch loop with the twine while holding the spool in hand, tensioning the twine. **2.** Tie a single overhand knot with the loop around the top end of the salami and pull tight. **3.** Place the loop over the tension holder. **4.** Lock the knot by tying a single overhand around the tensioned loop and pull tight. **5.** Now, run the twine vertically down the salami and wrap horizontally around its midsection. **6.** Tuck the twine under itself and continue vertically down the salami. As you get further and further down the salami it is vital to keep the tension with your thumb at the bottom of the salami, tightening with the thumb as needed.

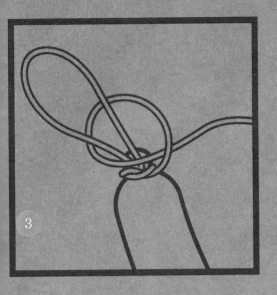

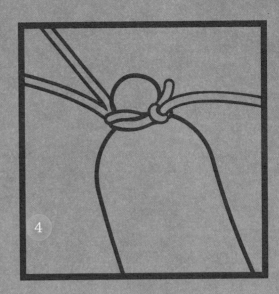

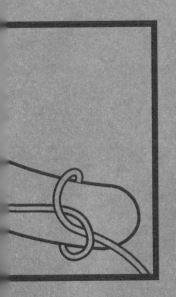

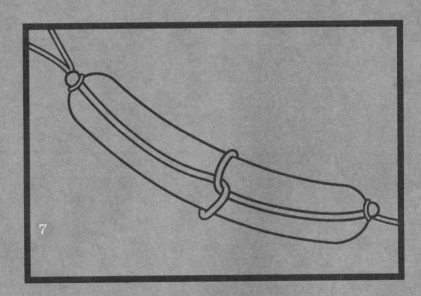

7. To finish, tie a single overhand knot around the taut end of the salami and pull tight. Lock in place with another overhand knot. Tie the next salami right into place behind the first, using the same technique without the loop. Tie three salamis in the chain (two if they are larger). Once they're tied, it is crucial that the fresh salamis be evenly perforated. Make sure to prick the ends where the salamis will stretch under weight. This step allows the air trapped in the salami to be vented under the pressure of the tying. If, after perforation, there are visible air pockets under the casing, re-perforate the area. I can't stress enough the importance of this step.

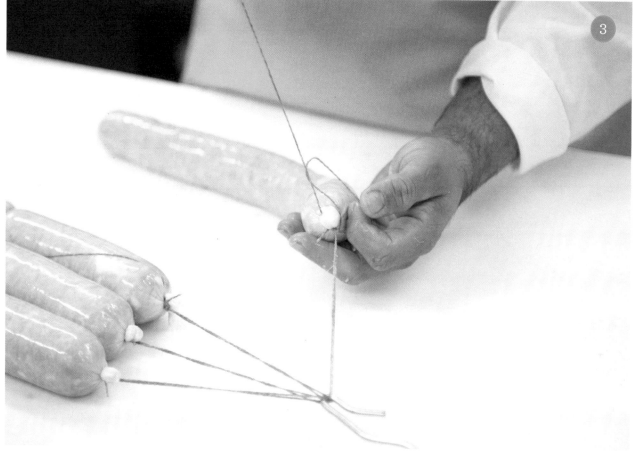

FERMENTATION

*I get to wake up at 2 am
and check on my salami. I am blessed!*

FERMENTATION

The fermentation process is the single most important factor to the overall taste and quality, and a mistake can lead to what Cristiano calls, "a deeply flawed salami." He explained that fermentation is really a short period where several vital steps happen almost simultaneously.

The temperature and humidity are primed for bacterial growth, and the sugars in the recipe provide food for the growing culture. As the bacteria begin to multiply and consume the sugars, there is a sudden drop in pH. It is this sudden lowering of pH that renders the salami completely safe to eat. The second step is the removal of water aiding in preservation.

It is crucial that this drop in pH happen as fast as possible, in 24 hours or less. The bacteria growth will continue as long as the food source is present, so overfeeding or over-fermenting will cause the salami to be too sour and acidic. In time, a properly fermented and aged salami will see its pH climb slightly back up, balancing the salami. Cristiano has been experimenting with different sugars as a food source for the bacteria, lowering the amount of dextrose and replacing it with a more complex sugar. This creates a dual-purpose food source in that half the sugar is consumed immediately and the other is consumed more slowly over a longer period. Fast acting and long lasting. This allows Cristiano to continually fine tune his fermentation process by adding another variable.

At the time of fermentation, the meat has a high water content, and the salt is pulling moisture from it. The case pricking gives the moisture being pulled out a place to vent. The high humidity also keeps the case permeable and soft to allow for proper respiration and drainage. As the salami plumps during fermentation, the pores created by pricking the skin wick out excess moisture, creating a more stable product. Strangely, it's like drying in a rain forest; the salt dries the salami from the inside out, and the high humidity keeps the case from dry sealing itself.

The actual start of the fermentation process begins with humidity at 99 percent and temperature between 72-75 degrees. In small curing cells, this extra humidity can be obtained by not drying the inside after a thorough cleaning, before bringing the salamis in. For the first ten hours the humidity must remain at a bare minimum of 75 percent, and the temperature must stay between 70-72 degrees. The humidity can be as high as 99 percent, but not below 75 percent. It is during this process that the bacteria consume the majority of their dextrose, providing the necessary drop in pH.

The second stage of the fermentation process is dramatically different. At this point, a hard drop in humidity needs to occur. For four or five hours, the humidity level needs to be 60 percent, and the temperature needs to be dropping slowly. This short period of drying and cooling removes excess water and begins preparing the salami for aging by slowing the bacteria activity. After four hours of low humidity, Cristiano begins steadily increasing the humidity. The general cooling trend occurs slowly for the next four to five days after fermentation, and by that time the temperature and humidity should be arriving at their stable aging rates, with humidity between 75-85 percent and temperatures between 55-60 degrees.

Cristiano checks on the salami repeatedly during the fermentation process, monitoring and tweaking constantly to prevent problems from escalating. This vigilance sets him apart from most of his peers. The years that he devoted to watching salami age have given him an uncanny ability to read them and correct them while maintaining an even and calm disposition.

· ·

I don't like to go fast when checking my salami. They have taught me patience.

· ·

MOLD

*First you have raw ugly meat, then you put
it into this room and poof — magic.*

———————

MOLD

"Without mold and bacteria, salumi making is more like drying," Cristiano explains. It is the life inside and outside the actual salami that does most of the work involved in proper aging. In this chapter, we will be talking specifically about the mold that forms on the outside of the casing and its different varieties.

Exterior mold plays several roles during the aging process, but its primary purpose is protection. It also acts as a gauge, showing the maker exactly what the salami is "feeling" in terms of relative humidity and temperature. Its final job is imparting flavor; mold gives salami a distinct signature taste.

It's crucial to understand that every step in this process relies on the one before it, and mold is the primary visual indicator of the process. By understanding the basic color variations and growth patterns, you will be able to maintain the right environmental conditions for the particular time in the salami's life cycle.

The first and most utilitarian purpose for mold growth is protection. Mold prohibits direct air contact, which dries and causes hardening. "Case hardening is the most common and most detrimental error in salumi making," warns Cristiano. Case hardening is normally a result of too little humidity, which occurs when the aging area is kept too cool. The cold pulls moisture from the air, drying and hardening the case, creating an impermeable membrane. Without permeability, the meat at the core of the salami remains raw and eventually sours, while the outer ring of meat turns a brown color and dries hard to the touch. This creates unbalanced salami, which may be edible but will probably result in an upset stomach.

Every step in this process relies on the one before it, and mold is the primary visual indicator of the process.

Colors

The basic colors of salami molds are white, blue, green, black, yellow, and red. Each color represents a particular environmental condition. It is interesting to note that Cristiano has refined his process so thoroughly that he seldom sees variations outside the realm of perfection. He corrects the smallest imperfection immediately, not allowing any problems to escalate. Cristiano will still see small spots of blue or green mold from time to time, but those salami are quickly moved to a higher airflow area of the aging cell and are quickly corrected. It is important to note that some "orangish" hues can appear on the casing once it goes into the refrigerator, but these are completely normal.

White: The baseline. "White is the mold color that we all shoot for," says Cristiano. "It is just perfect for good salami." White mold indicates the right pace and environmental conditions. If all the necessary conditions are met, it will begin to form very quickly. It will appear as small white specks scattered uniformly over the casing and then will blossom into a velvety coat. If you notice a pattern forming on the case, rotate to even the growth.

Green & Blue: Higher on the humidity scale are green and blue. These colors represent a significant rise in humidity. The higher humidity could be due to simple placement or an airflow issue. Increasing the space between the salamis can often be enough to correct the imbalance. These colors don't represent any real damage to the salami, internally; they just tell you the humidity is a bit higher than ideal. In fact, if you are going too far in one direction, it should be towards too much humidity. In most home cases, it is easier to remove humidity than to add it.

Black: Three-dimensional black growth can be pretty scary when you see it forming on something you plan to eat, but black mold is not actually an indication that the salami has gone bad. It is an indication, however, that the humidity is considerably higher than it should be and immediate correction is needed. If you are lucky enough to have a humidity control system, which allows you to directly control the humidity, drop the humidity and temperature by five percent and increase the airflow around the salami. Wipe off the black mold with a sterile wipe and monitor the temperature and humidity.

···

Red: it's dead.

···

It is possible that further changes will be required, but over-corrections can cause further instability. "The black color mold was more often seen in the old days," Cristiano tells me, "in old cellars with no airflow." In times of heavy or prolonged rain, the walls of the aging cellars would perspire, creating accelerated growth conditions that would often produce three-dimensional black mold.

Yellow: If you see yellow, it is usually because two salamis have been touching for long enough to begin developing bad anaerobic bacteria. This is the borderline phase in the bad mold/good mold balance. Depending on how extensively the bad mold has progressed, the salami may or may not be edible. Smell the infected area. Wipe with vinegar and smell again. If you are not sure, throw it out. If you decide to try to save these salami, monitor them very carefully and smell carefully for any trace of a bad odor. It's very important that these salami receive the most airflow possible, so if there is an area in your curing cell with more air movement, move them to that area.

Red: Once you see red, it's over. Throw it out, sterilize everything, and start from scratch. Remember, red: it's dead. At this point, the mold's progression has penetrated the salami past any point of repair, and eating it could do more than just give you bad indigestion. Red mold is relatively rare even if you are only halfway paying attention. This is an advanced case of bad mold growing to maturity, which most salumi artisans catch well before. Incidentally, Cristiano has no memory of ever actually seeing this mold.

A Note on Extreme Mold Color

Cristiano is an artisan who works with a degree of precision and attention to detail that most of us will never match. It is a credit to his great ability that certain flaws never develop during the production of his products. Problems that you and I might experience would seem like rare wild animal sightings to him.

I had the opportunity to ask Cristiano and his brother Andrea the same question regarding the more extreme forms of mold. With identical facial expressions, mannerisms, and even word choice, each replied, "I need to think about that. I do not remember the last time I saw this mold." Neither could recall any instances where they allowed a minor miscalculation to become a major issue. Their knowledge of extreme mold seems more based in legend than on actual experience, like a salumi maker's boogieman.

The red, yellow, and orange molds are primarily anaerobic, so they are most likely to develop where salami touch for extended periods. The contact between two salamis creates a surface devoid of oxygen, an environment where bad bacteria flourish. In other words, if you are making salami at home and you check it several times a day, you should have absolutely nothing to worry about. However, if you are making huge batches and cramming them into a small curing cell, you'll need to take extra care.

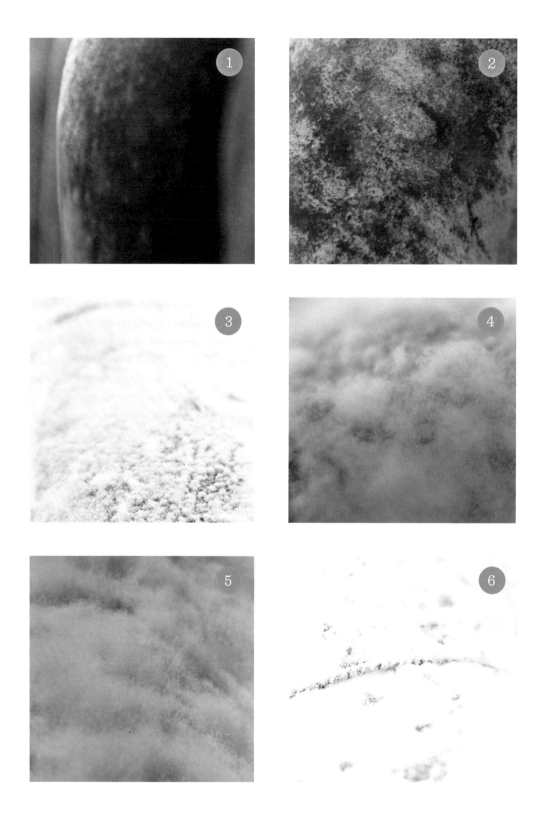

1. The mold is now clearly starting to take on three-dimensional growth.

2. The white mold continues growing, creating a slightly puffy appearance.

3. The white mold has thinly covered the entire salami.

4. The white mold has developed fully mature three-dimensional mold growth.

5. The evenly spread white specks begin filling in more and more slowly, enveloping the entire salami.

6. Initial colonation phase. Small white specks begin forming evenly.

Curing Cell Dynamics

Cristiano explained his particular take on humidity and temperature to me as I toured one of his aging rooms. He said that each cell has different settings, depending on the phase that each batch might be in. The larger aging cells are set up with the young salami on one end and the older, finishing salami on the other. He also told me that each cell and room had certain areas where mold would grow more or less than average.

These inconsistencies are usually airflow related. In areas of high air movement, the mold growth tends to be slower and more sporadic, while areas with less air movement tend to promote mold growth. Knowing these inconsistencies can be extremely helpful when you're trying to encourage slow mold growth or managing fast growth.

Cristiano relies heavily on the life in the air at his facility. The smell of aging pork and mold is palpable, filling your nose, your lungs, and even your pores. As soon as you walk into the building you are keenly aware of what function this building serves. The life that exists in the air is very valuable to his process, and Cristiano has worked extraordinarily hard to create an environment that allows his molds to grow with great efficiency. Air systems that suck in new air and expel old air actually remove this life from the chambers, lowering the overall levels. Cristiano mentioned that in his new facility, he wants a system that recycles most of the living air. This will give his new salami batches even easier access to the vital bacteria that will envelope and protect them.

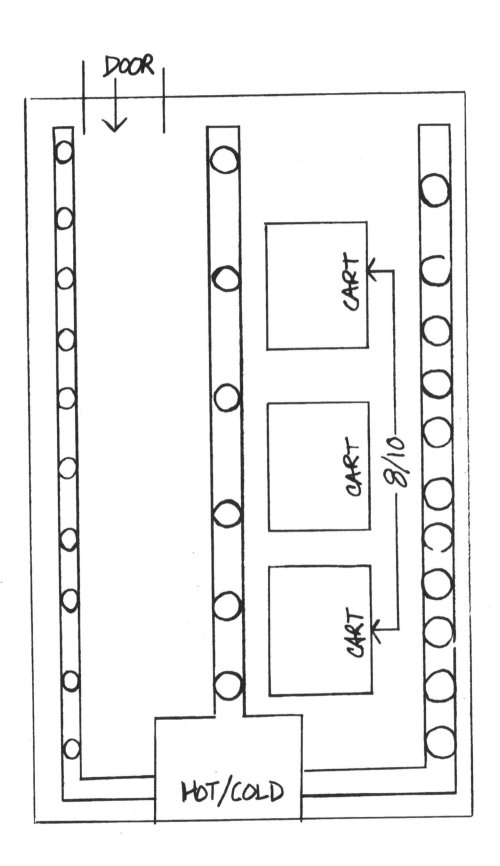

Common problems

Case hardening: Case hardening is the king of salami maladies. It occurs when the casing and the meat directly in contact with the case begin hardening and discoloring, sealing the permeability of the salami. When that happens, the interior of the salami is unable to age properly and stays wet and soft and often sours. Case hardening is caused by dry air. It is much better to have too much humidity than too little.

"I am always checking, at all hours, to make sure everything is right for the salami, so that little mistakes don't grow into big mistakes," says Cristiano.

Air pockets: Air pockets lead to oxidation and graying of the meat. Constant checking and correcting are necessary to ensure air is eliminated from all phases of production. Smaller stuffers are more prone to this problem and need to be well vented prior to stuffing. Cristiano's team thoroughly perforates the casings to allow the internal pressure to vent air pockets through the tiny fresh holes.

Over-fermentation: While it is possible to ferment the salami for too long, over-fermentation is usually a result of too much dextrose. Overfeeding the culture inside the salami is far more detrimental; it is the food source that allows the bacteria to keep reproducing, which creates sour, highly acidic, and indigestable salami. "The sugar is the food for the bacteria; too much food, too much fermentation." When salami are over-fermented, Cristiano uses the Italian word for rubber: "Ahh, it's *gomma*, you know, like a tire."

Sanitation: A sanitary environment is fundamental to the repeated production of salami. A salami maker has to think like a scientist. In order to properly culture bacteria, it is vital to eliminate competition to allow the desired strain to flourish. If harmful invasive bacteria are allowed to multiply, then the chance that they will beat out the desired bacteria is quite high. This is one area that Creminelli Fine Meats takes especially seriously. Intense industrial-style wash down and sanitation policies combined with an efficient production system ensure that Creminelli Fine Meats are impeccable.

Temperature: Temperature dictates the rates at which the bacteria will function. Below 50 degrees, life begins to slow drastically. Below 40 degrees, life crawls. At zero it stops. At 55 degrees, life continues on a steady pace. At 60, degrees life quickens its pace and has a higher metabolism.

Air-flow: Insufficient airflow is a common issue that usually results when salamis are too close or they touch. This creates an anaerobic environment between the salamis that will promote the growth of harmful bacteria and can spoil them if left uncorrected. Yellow or red mold is a common visual indicator of anaerobic activity. If airflow is too high, it will dry the salami and hinder exterior mold growth.

Cristiano's large batches create a sort of mutual support system among the sausages and enable him to rearrange his salami-loaded carts more freely. The salamis that require more humidity and less air-flow are placed in the center, while the opposite is true for salamis with ample or green/ blue mold growth or too much moisture.

The 17th Day

In Cristiano's world, day 17 is graduation day for salami. They have undergone a series of gradual climate changes leading up to this point that delicately shape the qualities of the salami. By day 17 they have balanced their pH and gained the flavors brought on by precise aging, so they are moved promptly into the RTE (ready to eat) room. Painstaking quality control standards ensure this room stays immaculately clean. This is the last stage before the salamis are prepped for shipping.

The salamis come out of the RTE room and are brushed briefly and rubbed with a small amount of rice flour. The rice flour has two real purposes: the first is to even the overall appearance of the salami, and the second is to keep the moisture levels balanced during shipping. Cristiano's salami usually leave the factory at about 21-23 days of age. This is important to keep in mind when purchasing salami, because just like any other living thing, salami has a life span that begins and ends.

Cutting and slicing a salami immediately begins draining its life at a rapid pace. It is best to consume one at a time so you don't have several uneaten halves drying out in your fridge. Understanding the different characteristics of a salami's age can add a new perspective to making and enjoying salami.

Day 17 is graduation day for salami.

9

HOW TO EAT

I like it best all by itself.

HOW TO EAT CREMINELLI SALAMI

Deciding when to eat a Creminelli salami is almost as important as what flavor you choose. Every day the salami will grow slightly more mature, becoming more and more condensed, wicking moisture from the inside out. This process creates a one-way path of aging, so timing the consumption of the salami within its taste peak is critical.

Most Italians tend to eat their salami a little younger and softer than the harder salami Americans are accustomed to.

I enjoy all phases of Creminelli salami, both the soft and the older, harder ones, but there is one particular stage that I personally find unbeatable. Right around 30 days, depending on your refrigerator, a special change occurs between the lean and the fat parts of the salami. The lean becomes firmer and begins exerting pressure on the plump, juicy portions of fat. When you chew, it feels like the small fat cubes explode in your mouth, creating an interesting contrast to the firm, lean portion. I urge you to experiment with different ages of salami to explore what textures you really enjoy. This will also give you some perspective on how the aging process directly affects the taste and mouth feel of salami.

How to peel a casing: If you've never removed the casing from a real Italian salami, you might find the process a bit intimidating. The directions are simple, but that doesn't mean it's easy. First decide how much salami you want to eat. With a sharp knife, slice through the skin vertically on a relatively flat salami surface, only as far down as you plan to eat. You always want uneaten portions of the salami to be protected by casing. Begin peeling at the edge of the sliced casing and continue pulling and peeling the casing away from the interior. As with all things important in life, practice makes perfect. The thickness of the slices should be dictated by the hardness of the salami; the harder the salami, the thinner the slices.

A Good Place to Start

I have only a few suggestions to help you enjoy salami. Salami is a simple pleasure that allows plenty of room for experimentation. Wine choices, cheese pairings, and the tremendous range of possible accompaniments should be exciting, not overwhelming. By using and trusting your palate, you can quickly build confidence in the ways you eat and serve salami. Eating salami is not typically a fine dining experience. In fact, it's usually pretty casual. For me it is a fantastic snack after work with a glass of red wine, usually consumed in the kitchen, right off the block or in my favorite chair. It's a simple and unassuming event, but when carried out just right, it can equal the experience of a four-Michelin-star restaurant.

Wines from Piemonte are an excellent starting point. Cristiano was lucky enough to grow up in this premier wine region of Italy, where even their table varietals show up on top wine lists all over the world. His products seem to have a natural rapport with these wines. They were both born of the same climate and culture, and their natural affinity for one another is unmistakable. The classic Barolos and Barbarescos are obvious choices for Cristiano, but he actually prefers the more pragmatic Piemonte wines made from the Barbera and Dolcetto grapes.

I like the Italian hard cheeses with Creminelli salami. The age and body hold up well to the deep aged flavor of the salami. Parmigiano-Reggiano has a subtle sweetness that balances the salinity of the salami yet is still robust enough to hold its own when paired. An aged Piave is a more delicate pairing and probably better suited to the Tartufo, while a Pecorino would be fantastic with a Casalingo or Cacciatore and some sliced figs and honey.

Even though I have been suggesting hard cheeses and red wines, they are absolutely not a rule. In the warmer months, I like a crisp, refreshing white, a Verdicchio or Langhe, and will often substitute the hard cheeses for a Burrata or a Stracchino, relatives of fresh mozzarella. Creminelli salami is made to be enjoyed in a personal manner, so honor your own distinct taste when choosing accompaniments.

In the following pages, we have included a few recipes made with Creminelli products. Adapted from family recipes and regional classics from Italy, they're meant to invoke the true spirit of salami culture. These are some delicious ways to use any leftover salami or end pieces, observing the Italian tradition of wasting nothing.

Cristiano's Salami Associations

BAROLO	Piemonte, my childhood.
CACCIATORE	Sweet.
FELINO	The oldest salami. The taste of tradition.
SOPRESSATA	Venice and garlic.
PICCANTE	Blue sea, long summer days. Spicy, full of life
TARTUFO	Sophisticated. Good for holidays. Real Italian taste.
CASALINGO	My family's salumificio. My home, my tradition.
WILD BOAR	Unique. Pine forest and mountains

10

COOKING WITH CREMINELLI FINE MEATS

I like to see the faces of people when they try the product. I want them to be stunned.

Mussels with Piccante Sausage and Tomato

2 Piccante sausages
Extra virgin olive oil
4 garlic cloves, sliced
6 heirloom cherry tomatoes, halved
1/4 cup white wine
1 cup of San Marzano tomato liquid
1/4 cup clam juice
Salt to taste
2 dozen live mussels, debearded
Parsley
Chili flakes
1 lemon, sliced

Heat a stainless steel frying pan over high heat. Remove the sausage from the casing and break into approximately one-inch pieces. Drizzle olive oil into the hot pan and brown the small sausage pieces. Once they're browned on both sides, remove sausage from the pan and set aside. Add the sliced garlic and the tomato halves to the pan and sauté for two minutes. Deglaze the pan with the white wine, making sure to cook off all the alcohol. Add the tomato liquid and clam juice, season with salt, and stir thoroughly. Cook over medium high heat until the broth comes to a boil and reduces slightly. Add the cleaned mussels to the boiling broth and toss, coating them evenly. Cover the pan and cook on high heat for 2-3 minutes or until the shells open. Garnish with torn parsley, chili flakes, and lemon.

Creminelli Sopressata Stuffed Artichokes

Sea salt
4 lemons
6 medium fresh artichokes
1 cup breadcrumbs
1 cup grated Parmigiano-Reggiano
1 cup picked flat leaf parsley
1/2 link of Creminelli Sopressata
1 stick unsalted butter
8 cloves garlic, crushed
Extra virgin olive oil
Chili flakes
4 Tbl. caper berries or capers
1 cup white wine

Fill large pot with water and bring to a boil. Add sea salt until the salinity is close to that of seawater. Slice two whole lemons and juice and add to water. The acidulated water will help prevent oxidation, and the salt water will help preserve the green color. While waiting for the water to boil, begin cleaning the artichokes by clipping the pointed ends of leaves with scissors all the way around and cutting off the top inch of the artichokes with a very sharp, or even serrated, knife. Trim and peel the stems, saving them to add flavor. Mix the breadcrumbs, cheese, and parsley in a small mixing bowl and set aside. Peel approximately 1/2 of a Creminelli salami and slice into 1/8 inch rounds and set aside.

In a deep-edged saucepan bring 1/4 stick of butter and the 8 crushed garlic cloves over medium heat until garlic is toasted lightly. Once tender, remove the artichokes from the water. Do not drain the artichokes completely; the residual blanching water will help the cooking process and add flavor. Once they've cooled slightly, gently open the leaves to allow for easier stuffing of the breadcrumb mixture and salami slices. Sprinkle the breadcrumb mixture on top and into the opened leaves of the artichoke. Place the salami slices into dressed artichokes evenly. Each choke should have 6-8 slices of salami, depending on the size. Add the juice of one lemon, a drizzle of olive oil, chili flakes, capers or caper berries, and parsley over the entire dish. Pour 1/2 to 1 cup of good quality white wine to the bottom of the pan. Continue sautéing on stovetop until alcohol evaporates, then finish under the broiler for about 30 seconds.

Fresh Sausage Stuffing

1/4 cup Extra virgin olive oil
3 links Creminelli Piccante fresh sausage
2 crusty baguettes
4 cloves of garlic
2 medium yellow onions, chopped
4 celery stalks with leaves, washed
1 cup red wine
2 or 3 whole eggs
1 large bunch Italian parsley, chopped
1 cup Parmigiano-Reggiano, freshly grated
2 Tbl. fennel seeds
1 cup chicken stock
Salt and pepper to taste

Place enamel skillet or large saute pan on stove, over medium heat. Decase the sausage and break into 1-2 inch pieces and cube or tear the loaves of bread into just slightly larger chunks. Add the sausage to the hot pan with a drizzle of olive oil and brown sausage on both sides. Add the garlic, onions, and celery, then sweat lightly, taking care to scrape the bottom of the pan, loosening the browned bits. Add the red wine and deglaze lightly. Remove from heat and add to mixing bowl with bread, parsley, Parmigiano- Reggiano, and the fennel seeds. Crack two eggs into a small bowl and whisk quickly with fork or whisk. Pour the egg over the cubed bread, cheese, and sausage mixture and toss thoroughly to incorporate. The recipe is now ready to be stuffed into a prepared bird. If baking in a dish, add chicken stock to prevent drying and cover to prevent over-browning, if needed.

Panzanella

2 Creminelli fresh sausages
1 loaf crusty Italian or French bread, large cubes
(If crust is thick, thin accordingly.)
1 medium red onion, halved and shaved
Arugula or fresh greens
Capers, rinsed and coarsely chopped
1/2 cup white wine
3 Tbl. white wine vinegar
Small handful flat leaf parsley
Chili flake
5 garlic cloves, minced
1/2 extra virgin olive oil
Balsalmic vinegar, drizzle
3 Tbl. chopped thyme
Shaved Parmigiano-Reggiano

This slightly warm salad is a wonderful light yet satisfying version of a traditional Panzanella, incorporating Creminelli sausage. The use of old bread to extend a meal is a common practice throughout the world, but Italians excel creatively in their ability to conjure entirely new and mouth-watering meals from leftovers. This salad is a slightly more luxurious version of the standard, with its addition of Creminelli sausage.

Begin by heating a heavy-bottomed pan on medium-high heat and preheating the oven to 400 degrees. While the pan is getting hot, begin roughly cubing the bread into 1-2 inch pieces. Place bread cubes in a large metal mixing bowl. Remove the sausage from the casing and break into 2-3 inch pieces. Drizzle a small amount of olive oil in the hot pan and start browning the sausage slowly, rendering the fat. Be careful not to burn or scorch the oil and fat. After browning it on all sides, remove the sausage from the pan and set aside. Do not discard the oil in the pan. Add the minced garlic and chopped thyme to the bread bowl. While the oil is still hot in the pan, pour it over the bread cubes and toss the bread, garlic, and thyme to mix and coat thoroughly (adding more olive oil if necessary). It is important to use the sponge-like structure of the bread to soak up the garlicky oil and thyme on the bottom of the bowl. Think of using the bread to clean the bowl. Spread the coated bread cubes flat on a sheet tray and bake in the oven till golden brown. In a small saucepan, heat the wine and white wine vinegar until boiling and add the sliced red onions. Toss thoroughly and remove from heat. To plate the salad, begin by putting a handful of warm toasted bread cubes per person in a large mixing bowl. Add the sausage pieces, parsley, chili flake, chopped capers, arugula, olive oil, balsamic vinegar, and scalded onions, and toss gently. The gentle heat from the sausage and toasted bread softens the arugula while the bread absorbs the liquid. Finish with shaved Parmigiano-Reggiano and black pepper.

Risotto di Piemonte

1/2 cup Barolo salami from end pieces, cubed
Extra virgin olive oil
1 clove garlic
2 sprigs thyme, picked
3 cups of Carnaroli, Baldo, or Arborio rice
2-3 quarts chicken stock
3 sage leaves
Salt to taste
1 cup Parmigiano-Reggiano, freshly grated
Copper sauce pot
Wooden or high heat plastic spoon

I learned this classic Piemontese recipe while visiting the restaurant of local reigning risotto legends in a small town outside Bra. Our class had driven about five or six hours north to check out several destinations in the area, when we stopped to try the "best traditional risotto in Piemonte." We had already been to an amazing pre-war wooden rice factory powered by water from the irrigation cells, and we were eager to watch this elegant grain come full circle. The recipe here is almost identical to the one we tasted, except for the fact that I substitute Creminelli Barolo salami instead of the cockscomb called for in the original, which might not appeal to everyone.

Heat the copper pot for 2 minutes on medium high, then add the cubed salami ends and a small drizzle of olive oil. Sauté briefly. Add the whole garlic clove and picked thyme and toast lightly. Next, add the rice and stir constantly, coating all the grains with rendered salami fat and olive oil. Toast the rice for two minutes, stirring constantly, until the rice begins changing its levels of translucence. At this point the ladling of stock begins. The idea is to use only small amounts of liquid at a time, ensuring that the rice is cooked by the vaporized stock, not boiled. The constant stirring will build the starch, giving the risotto a creamy finish. The next 12-16 minutes will be quite strenuous and will require stirring stamina. Don't give up. Continue ladling small amounts of stock and stirring until the rice reaches the right bite for your taste. Season with salt and pepper and grated Parmigiano-Reggiano and fold through. Add enough liquid to attain the desired consistency and garnish with julienned sage and shaved or grated Parmigiano-Reggiano.

kitchen cloth
no.5027   color : n g
45 X 65 cm linen 100%

Ribolita

3 red onions, diced small
2 leeks, diced small
8 stalks celery, diced small
2 large carrots, diced small
8 Creminelli salami end pieces, or half a whole salami, sliced thin
and minced
9 cloves garlic, chopped
Bouquet garni
1 can San Marzano tomatoes
1.5 quarts leftover cooked white beans
2 quarts chicken stock
Parsley
1 day-old baguette, cubed, tossed with oil, thyme, and garlic then
toasted
Shaved Parmigiano-Reggiano
The rind of Parmigiano-Reggiano

This traditional Italian soup is another devastatingly delicious meal made from leftovers. Its vegetable-heavy base makes the soup very nutritious, but the added accent of pork makes it extra special. The incorporation of the minced end pieces of Creminelli salami is a fantastic way to use those little pieces that are hard to serve. The toasted day-old bread and Parmigiano-Reggiano rind give the soup an added salty dimension. Place a large rondeau on low heat. While waiting for the pot to get hot, begin by dicing the onions, leeks, celery, carrots, garlic cloves, parsley, and salami and put into a large bowl. The rondeau should be quite hot by the time you finish chopping. Drizzle a generous amount of olive oil into the rondeau and then transfer the contents of the mixing bowl to the pot and sweat the mixture till tender.

Preheat the oven to 350-400 degrees. After sweating the mix, add the can of whole peeled San Marzano tomatoes and season. Mix thoroughly and cook for five minutes. Add the chicken stock, bouquet garni, and Parmigiano-Reggiano rind and cook for one hour on low heat. Take two cups of the white beans and puree with two ladles of the soup, add the pureed beans and whole beans to the soup, and cook for 25 minutes. Season to taste and remove the bouquet garni and the Parmigiano-Reggiano rind. Toss the bread cubes in oil, fresh garlic, thyme, and shredded Parmigiano-Reggiano and toast in the oven until golden brown. Ladle into warm bowls and garnish with torn basil, more shaved Parmigiano-Reggiano, and toasted bread.

Salumi Making Resources

FARMS

CHRISTIANSEN FARM — Vernon, UT
christiansenfarm.com

BALLARD'S FARM — Wayne, WV
ballardsfarm.com

COLEMAN NATURAL FOODS— Golden, CO
colemannatural.com

GUM CREEK FARMS — Roopville, GA
facebook.com/pages/Roopville-GA/Gum-
Creek-Farms/101155389215

CURING CELLS

FRIGOMECCANICA
www.frigomeccanica.it

TRAVAGLINI
www.travaglini.it

TYING STRING

HEMP BASICS
www.hempbasics.com/shop/ecom-catshow/
Hemp-Twine-and-Cord.html

NATURAL CASING

BUTCHER AND PACKER
www.butcher-packer.com

KOCH EQUIPMENT
www.kochequipment.com

MEAT PROCESSING PRODUCTS

MEAT PROCESSING PRODUCTS
www.meatprocessingproducts.com

FABIO LEONARDI
www.fabioleonardi.it/meat-grinders.html

ARREDO INOX
www.arredoinox.it/default.asp?id=E76NO71KMJ

ARRETURCOM
www.arreturcom.it

CAVALLI
www.cavallimpm.it

INOX MECCANICA
www.inoxmeccanica.it

A note from Cristiano

Ho passato l'intera mia vita facendo questo lavoro che mi ha sempre regalato grandi soddisfazioni e per il quale non ho mai faticato un singolo minuto, per me è sempre stato un piacere ed un onore. Già da piccolo, grazie alla infinita pazienza e amore di mio padre , non avevo dubbi riguardo al mio futuro: volevo poter anch'io creare questo piccolo capolavoro che a tavola da molta gioia a parecchie persone.

Poi ho trovato mia moglie, la compagna che mi da la carica necessaria ad ogni singola giornata ma soprattutto la mia coscienza; e lei ha trovato me (molte volte mi ricorda divertita che quand'era piccola diceva ai suoi genitori: " Da grande voglio sposare un uomo capace di fare i salami". Per lei erano il cibo più buono della terra !) e dopo alcuni anni la mia bellissima bambina. Forse avevo tutto ciò che volevo nella vita ma non mi sentivo "completo" e non ne capivo il motivo.

Agli inizi del 2000 ho incontrato i miei futuri partner (Chris Bowler e Jared Lynch) che mi hanno dato l'idea di iniziare nuovamente tutto qui negli USA. Era una grande sfida ma ho accettato. Ora mi trovo qui con questa fantastica azienda contornato da fantastiche persone e ho forse trovato quel qualcosa che mancava alla mia vita: il profondo senso di tranquillità che mi da questo grande paese. Spero che leggendo questo libro possiate comprendere a fondo la passione che lega un artigiano al proprio prodotto e auguro a tutti voi una vita piena com'è stata la mia sino ad ora.

I have spent my entire life in this work that always gives me such great satisfaction. For me, making salami is not a job, but a simple way of life. It is always a pleasure and an honor to craft such a beautiful food. From the time when I was a little boy, thanks to the infinite patience and love of my father, in my mind, there was never any doubt about my future: I wanted to be able to create these little "masterpieces" that make people so very happy at the dinner table.

Then, I found my wife, a partner who was able to give me the inspiration I need every day, but above all my conscience. At the same time, she found me: She remembers, amusingly, when she was really young she used to tell her parents, "When I grow up I want to marry a guy who can make salami." For her it was the best food in the whole world! Then, after some years we had our beautiful daughter. Maybe I had everything I wanted in my life but I felt myself "incomplete" and I didn't understand why.

In the beginning of the year 2000, I found my future business partners, (Chris Bowler and Jared Lynch) and they gave me the idea to start everything again in the USA. It was a big challenge, but I accepted! Now I'm here with a fantastic company, surrounded by fantastic people, and I think I found the missing part of my life: the deep sense of peace that I receive from this great country.

I hope that you who read this book may be able to understand the passion that "ties" this artisan to his own creation, and may your life be as full as mine.

About PC Press

Housed in an old 1940s factory building on Bennett Street in Atlanta lies a small school with an enormous heart. Here, an ambitious corps of graduate-level communication arts students conceive and create the near impossible every day, year-round.

Student designers, interactive designers, art directors, copywriters, illustrators, and photographers work together in classes and on projects for clients such as Coca-Cola, The Cartoon Network, The Weather Channel, and Apple. They birth ad campaigns, restaurant concepts, websites, children's books, museum installments, corporate identities, and an endless list of Other Things.

Perhaps there is no school in the world more defined by the people inside it, or by the spirit, energy, and imagination that they embody. In an environment that offers no dorm or cafeteria, no student lounge, and a sketchy vending machine that only works if you stroke it a certain way, these kids discover their most resourceful and ingenious selves. They flourish under the expert guidance of seasoned professionals who teach them the rules and how to break them, who teach them how to make new rules. Their award-winning projects are published in CMYK, Creativity, Graphis, and American Photographer, to name a few.

This past year, Portfolio Center launched PC Press, a publishing arm that gives our students an unusual opportunity. We have everything we need, in-house, including the talent required, to create beautiful books, from concept through production. Meat. Salt. Time. was PC Press's first full-steam venture, and it has taken students to Salt Lake City, Utah, and to Biella, Italy.

It has been a most interesting learning process, too, and not just related to publishing. The CEO's office was turned into a butcher shop so the designer could learn to break down a pig. The photographer learned more about charcuterie and its implements than he ever dreamed of—or wanted to. Even the editor had an epiphany when, after being buried in various incarnations of the text for months, it finally hit her that, "Hey, salami is never cooked!"

Everyone involved in this project now has a greater appreciation for tradition, craftsmanship, hospitality, and pigs. Everyone has practiced collaboration through its entire cycle: honeymoon, contempt, and true partnership--at times scary, with so many knives involved. It has been an immersive experience and an unforgettable one.

This is Portfolio Center.

Notes Section: